SPACE TECH

EARTH SATELLITES

by ALLAN MOREY

EPIC

BELLWETHER MEDIA • MINNEAPOLIS, MN

EPIC BOOKS are no ordinary books. They burst with intense action, high-speed heroics, and shadows of the unknown. Are you ready for an Epic adventure?

This edition first published in 2018 by Bellwether Media, Inc.

No part of this publication may be reproduced in whole or in part without written permission of the publisher. For information regarding permission, write to Bellwether Media, Inc., Attention: Permissions Department, 5357 Penn Avenue South, Minneapolis, MN 55419.

Library of Congress Cataloging-in-Publication Data

Names: Morey, Allan.
Title: Earth Satellites / by Allan Morey.
Description: Minneapolis, MN : Bellwether Media, Inc., 2018. | Series: Epic. space tech | Audience: Ages 7-12. |
   Includes bibliographical references and index.
Identifiers: LCCN 2016059021 (print) | LCCN 2017016276 (ebook) | ISBN 9781626176997 (hardcover : alk. paper) |
   ISBN 9781681034294 (ebook) | ISBN 9781618912824 (paperback : alk. paper)
Subjects: LCSH: Artificial satellites–Juvenile literature. | Scientific satellites–Juvenile literature.
Classification: LCC TL796.3 (ebook) | LGC TL796.3 .M67 2018 (print) | DDC 629.43–dc23
LC record available at https://lccn.loc.gov/2016059021

Editor: Nathan Sommer   Designer: Steve Porter

Printed in the United States of America, North Mankato, MN.

TABLE OF CONTENTS

EARTH SATELLITE AT WORK!

It is February 2013. A rocket carries the Landsat 8 into space. This satellite will circle Earth 14 times a day! It will take thousands of pictures. The pictures will help scientists study **climate change**.

rocket carrying Landsat 8

Landsat 8

WHAT ARE EARTH SATELLITES?

Earth satellites are any objects that **orbit** Earth. The moon is one of many natural satellites. There are also thousands of human-made satellites circling the planet. These were sent into space using rockets.

The satellite sends a signal.

1

Satellites have many jobs. Some send **signals** that allow phones and televisions to work. Others check the weather. Satellites also control **GPS**. GPS helps people get places.

SPACE LAB!

The International Space Station is the largest human-made satellite.

PARTS OF EARTH SATELLITES

The bus is the body of a satellite. It holds most of the machine's important parts. **Thrusters** on the bus help the satellite change directions. **Solar panels** connected to the bus power the satellite.

solar panel

thrusters

bus

Satellites often have cameras and **telescopes**. Some take pictures to map and study Earth's features. Others take photos of the sun and faraway stars. These help scientists better understand the **universe**.

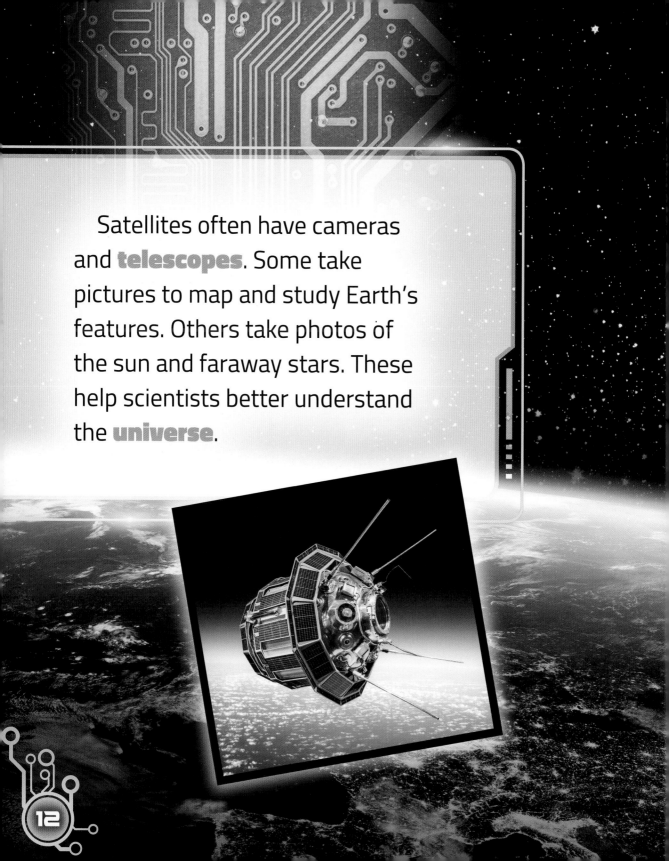

IDENTIFY THE MACHINE

Earth satellite

solar panels

thruster

bus

EARTH SATELLITE MISSIONS

In 1957, the **Soviet Union** launched Sputnik 1. It was the first human-made satellite. It communicated with Earth through **radio waves**. This opened the door to future space **exploration**!

Mars exploration

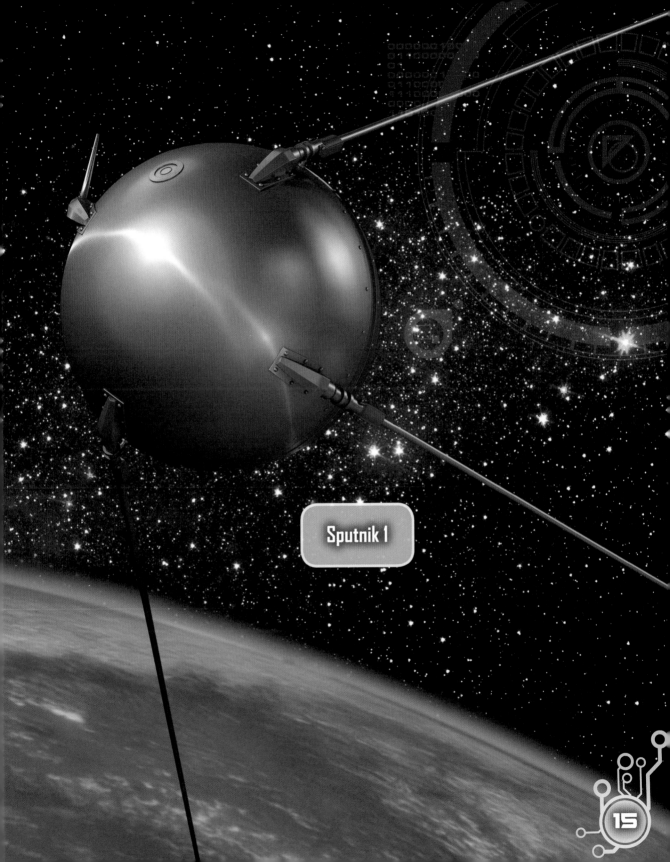

Sputnik 1

CloudSat

NASA launched its first satellite in 1958. Explorer 1 studied the radiation around Earth. Since then, NASA has launched hundreds of satellites. One example is CloudSat. This satellite is used to study clouds.

FLOATING AROUND!

The U.S. Navy launched Vanguard 1 in 1958. It is the oldest satellite still in orbit around Earth.

Today, satellites help people more than ever. They track the weather. They also help people stay in touch. Thanks to satellites, life is much easier!

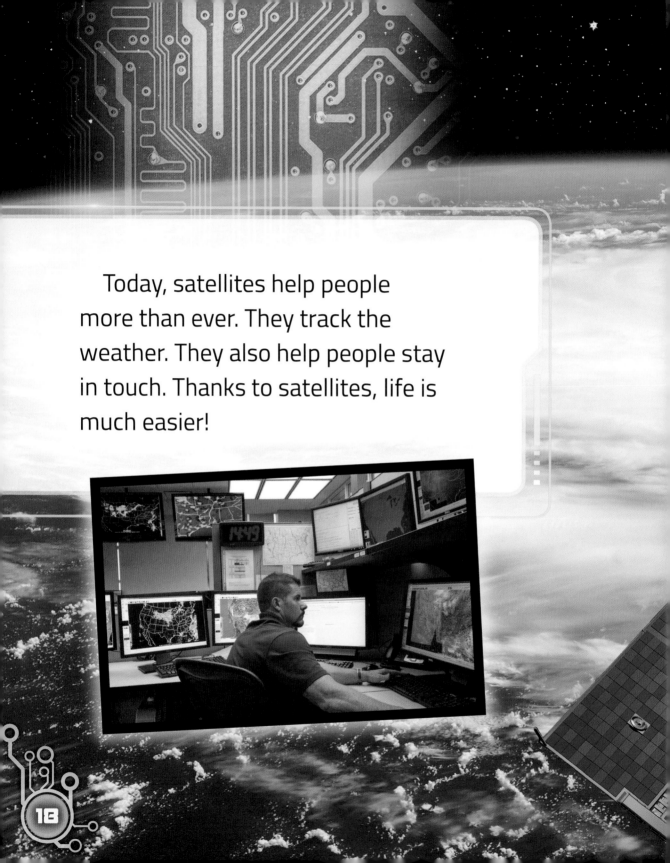

satellite
tracking
weather

GOES-16 SATELLITE SPECS

images from
GOES-16

NAME: GOES-16

Geostationary Operational Environmental Satellite

- **mission:** to quickly collect weather data to warn about storms and severe weather
- **first time in space:** 2016

- **speed:** completes its orbit of Earth in 24 hours; because it moves at the same speed as Earth, it remains fixed over the same spot.

- **length:** 20 feet (6.1 meters)
- **width:** 18.4 feet (5.6 meters)
- **height:** 12.8 feet (3.9 meters)

- **location in space:** orbiting Earth from 22,300 miles (35,888 kilometers) away, directly above the equator

GLOSSARY

climate change—the long-term change in Earth's weather patterns

exploration—the act of traveling through an unfamiliar area to learn more about it

GPS—short for global positioning system, a system that tells people where they are

NASA—National Aeronautics and Space Administration; NASA is a U.S. government agency responsible for space travel and exploration.

orbit—to circle around an object

radiation—energy waves

radio waves—types of waves used to send information over long distances

signals—messages or information sent by satellites

solar panels—devices that collect sunlight and turn it into energy

Soviet Union—a former country in eastern Europe and western Asia made up of 15 smaller republics or states

telescopes—devices used for seeing distant objects, especially those in outer space

thrusters—small engines on a spacecraft used to control its direction in outer space

universe—all of existence

TO LEARN MORE

AT THE LIBRARY

Parker, Steve. *The Story of Space: Satellites*. Mankato, Minn.:
A+ Smart Apple Media, 2016.

Poolos, Christine. *What Is an Object in the Sky?* New York, N.Y.:
Britannica Educational Publishing, 2015.

VanVoorst, Jenny Fretland. *Artificial Satellites*. Minneapolis, Minn.:
Pogo, 2017.

ON THE WEB

Learning more about Earth satellites
is as easy as 1, 2, 3.

1. Go to www.factsurfer.com.

2. Enter "Earth satellites" into the search box.

3. Click the "Surf" button and you will see a
list of related web sites.

With factsurfer.com, finding more information is just a click away.

INDEX